SNOOKER

POOL & BILLIARDS

Peter Arnold

Kingfisher Books

Introduction

Snooker is a game of skill and precision. Like most games and sports, you need lots of practice to gain the accuracy needed to win regularly.

This book explains many of the basic techniques involved and should help you to success.

Best of luck on the table!

Kingfisher Books, Grisewood and Dempsey Ltd,
Elsley House, 24–30 Great Titchfield Street,
London W1P 7AD

First published in hard cover in 1987 by Kingfisher Books

Reprinted 1988

© Grisewood & Dempsey Limited 1987

BRITISH LIBRARY CATALOGUING IN PUBLICATION DATA
Arnold, Peter,
   Snooker and billiards—(Kingfisher
   factbooks)
   1. Billiards—Juvenile literature
   2. Pool (Game)—Juvenile literature
   3. Snooker—Juvenile literature
   I. Title
   794.7′2   GV891

   ISBN 0-86272-293-4

Printed in Portugal by Printer Portuguesa
Phototypeset by Southern Positives and Negatives (SPAN), Lingfield, Surrey

Contents

1: The story of snooker

Snooker is a fairly new game, which was invented just over 100 years ago. Before then, outdoor games were popular, such as croquet, where balls were hit through small hoops. In the 15th century, a version of croquet was moved indoors and played on a table. This game was called billiards – the stick, or cue, was the 'billiard'.

The earliest mention of billiards was in France, in 1429, but the first public billiards room was in the Piazza, Covent Garden, in London during the early 19th century.

As the years passed, other games were devised for the billiards table, including 'pyramids'. This used a batch of red balls in a triangle like the one used in present-day snooker. It was a betting game. Any player who potted a red ball into a table pocket collected a stake from the other players. Another game, called 'life pool', used various coloured balls.

▶ *This engraving of 1900 shows a French billiards hall. Lady players, then and now, are the exception rather than the rule round the table.*

The game of snooker was created by combining billiards with the red balls of pyramids and the coloured balls of life pool. Credit for it goes to a British regiment, based at Jabalpur, India, in 1875. They supplied the name too.

Hardened soldiers nicknamed recruits at the Royal Military Academy 'snookers'. Snookers didn't know much, and when one of his colleagues missed a shot, the Colonel of the regiment teasingly called him a snooker – then suggested it was a good name for the new game!

At first, billiards players played snooker for a change and a rest, but it wasn't long before snooker was being played seriously. Championships were started in 1916, and the first World Professional Championship was played eleven years later, with the final in Birmingham.

In 1927, Joe Davis became the first World Champion. He remained World Champion until he retired in 1947. By then, snooker was more popular than billiards. Even so, there were only a few professional players, and snooker was hardly a popular sport compared to cricket or soccer.

In 1969 a new television channel, BBC2, broadcast in colour for the first time. BBC2 was looking for a new sport to show, suitable for colour TV – and snooker was chosen for a series called *Pot Black*.

The programme was a success. With success, came sponsorship money. The World Championship, which had almost died through lack of interest in the 1950s and 1960s, attracted attention again. TV audiences went up and up. In 1985, 18.5 million viewers watched Dennis Taylor win the World Championship. This was the largest viewing figure for a British after-midnight TV show. In the last ten years, TV snooker has increased from less than 20 to over 300 hours per year – more than two weeks of TV programming!

Professional players have their own association, the World Professional Billiards and Snooker Association. The WPBSA organizes all pro-events. It acts as a snooker policeman too, with

▲ Pot Black *was the first TV snooker programme. The game is now shown on TV in many countries all over the world. The bright colours of balls and table make snooker a great choice for colour television.*

powers to fine or suspend players if they break the rules.

The world governing body is the Billiards and Snooker Control Council. The BSCC makes and changes the rules. The World Championship itself is organized by yet another body, the International Billiards and Snooker Federation.

Snooker has spread round the world now. In Australia, Channel 10 TV shows the most popular event, the Winfield Masters. Snooker exploded in popularity in Canada during the 1970s – and three Canadians won the World Team Classic in 1982. They were Cliff Thorburn, Kirk Stevens and Bill Werbeniuk.

South Africa has been a snooker stronghold since the 1930s and Malta has produced some outstanding players. British soldiers introduced the game there during World War II. Surprisingly, in India, where the game started, snooker has taken a long time to overtake billiards.

The stronghold of the game is still in Britain. Only twice has the professional champion come from

Prize Money

Top player

10th player

20th player

35th player

50th player

Total amounts for the top ten players

1983-4	1984-5	1985-6
£147,200	£182,500	£244,333
£25,000	£56,628	£69,230
£11,300	£22,250	£27,940
£4,450	£10,000	£12,123
£2,175	£4,900	£8,063
£517,650	£1,011,170	£1,277,300

any other part of the world. In 1952, Australian Horace Lindrum won (but the British had withdrawn). In 1980, Canadian Cliff Thorburn took the title.

But the game does have international appeal – 22 countries supplied entrants for the 1984 World Amateur Championships. A 'first-timer' in this series was the United States and the winner was Omprakanash Agrawal from India, the first amateur champion who wasn't English or Welsh. Maybe future champions will come from the USA or Hong Kong . . .

▲ *This chart shows how prize money has increased in the last three seasons. The figures are the tournament earnings for the whole season. Players can make even more money from exhibitions and commercial sponsorships.*

2: The equipment

The only piece of equipment a player might own is a cue. The top players are very possessive about their cues, often using a favourite one all their life. If you are young, you need not rush to choose yours, however, since the length of your cue usually depends on your height.

When the cue is stood on the floor, the tip should be about 25 mm below your shoulder. The rules state that a cue must be at least 910 mm (3 ft) long.

A cue has various parts. The main wooden parts are the shaft, usually made of maple or ash. It is attached to the butt, made of ebony or a similar hard wood. A metal ferrule and a leather tip are attached to the end of the cue. Tips are glued on, often with a specially made glue wafer.

You should choose a cue which feels well balanced, with its point of balance about where the 'points'

▶ A cue is made up of various parts – the butt, the shaft, the ferrule and the tip. The length of the cue you use depends on your height. A two-piece cue unscrews in the middle.

The Cue

Length at least 910mm (3ft)

Shaft

Tip made of leather

Ferrule made of brass

Two part cues screw together here

The 'points' of a cue

Correct length of cue reaches just below shoulders

Butt

of the butt meet the shaft. It should not be rigid, but it should not be too whippy either. If you hold the butt and smack the shaft against the other hand, it should vibrate slightly.

Most cues weigh between 450 and 500 g (16–18 oz). Few professionals would use anything lighter than 450 g (16 oz), but the main thing is that the cue should be comfortable to use.

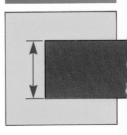

▲ A snooker table rests on a bed of slate which can be 50 mm deep.

The tip is another personal matter, and depends on a player's 'feel'. Standard tips are of 10 mm, 11 mm, or about 9.5 mm ($\frac{3}{8}$ in).

The tip should be gently domed, and be firm but not hard. It should compress slightly when the cue ball is struck. If the tip is too hard, the ball will skid away and be difficult to control. If the tip is too soft, it will make a soggy impact.

You can replace a tip at home with contact glue or a gelatine wafer. Tips can be shaped with a sharp, fine file. File backwards from the tip towards the butt. When you are playing, chalk the tip regularly and lightly to stop it slipping.

▶ A snooker table with its markings. The size of the table and the positions of the spots are specified by the Billiards and Snooker Control Council.

The table

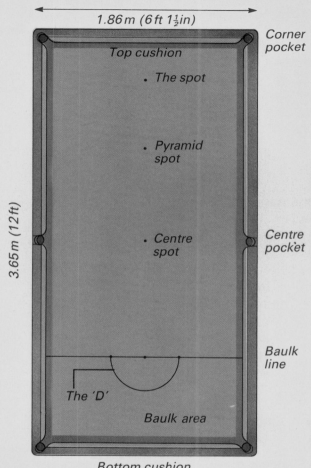

1.86 m (6 ft 1½ in)

Corner pocket

Top cushion

. The spot

. Pyramid spot

. Centre spot

Centre pocket

3.65 m (12 ft)

Baulk line

The 'D'

Baulk area

Bottom cushion

Two-piece cues are popular, even with professionals. The two pieces are screwed together at the centre. A neat refinement is an extra long butt end, giving an extended cue to use with the rest (see page 40). Two-piece cues are easier to take from place to place.

The other equipment needed, such as balls, chalk and rests, usually belongs with the table, so is provided by the snooker club or hall.

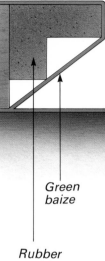

Green baize

Rubber cushion

The table itself is a complex piece of equipment. Championship tables are specially assembled at the venue to make sure the conditions of play are perfect.

The 'bed' of the table is made of slate up to 50 mm (2 in) thick. The cushions are made of rubber. The cloth is green, to imitate grass, from the old days of croquet. It has a nap which runs from baulk end to the top end, which you can feel if your stroke it. Tournament tables are ironed every day. The nap can have an effect on spin shots.

Manufacturers guard the secret of blending the different wools which go into making the cloth – the best wools make the best

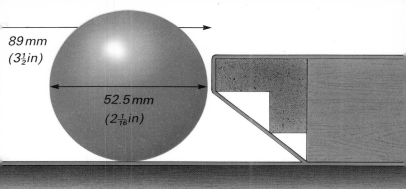

89 mm
(3½in)

52.5 mm
(2 1/16 in)

playing surfaces. The size of the pockets are specified by the BSCC and must be 89 mm (3½ in) wide.

The first balls were made from wood, then from ivory. Luckily the invention of plastics came just in time to save the world's elephants from the snooker boom – ivory comes from elephant tusks. Balls are now made of resin compound, and are carefully made in sets so that each ball in a set weighs the same as the others. Each ball is 52.5 mm (2 1/16 in) in diameter.

▲ *A snooker ball can drop into a pocket with nearly 37 mm (1½in) to spare.*

3: Basic rules of the game

At the beginning of a **frame** (a game) of snooker, the balls are set up on their spots as shown on the right. The pyramid of 15 reds is as near to the pink ball as possible without touching it.

The first player 'breaks off' by placing the white **cue ball** anywhere in the **D** and playing towards the reds. Each player (or pair of players in a 'doubles' match) has a turn (or **break**) alternately. A break continues until a player fails to score with a shot, or commits a foul.

To build a break, a player must first **pot** a red ball (one point) into a pocket, then any colour he likes. The term 'colour' in snooker applies to the yellow, green, brown, blue, pink, and black balls – not the reds. Should he pot a colour, he scores according to its value (shown on page 18) and then must pot another red. Play continues like this – red, colour,

▼ *The first player starts by hitting the white cue ball from any part of the D. Most players aim to just 'kiss' an outer red, bouncing the white off the top cushion, back towards the D.*

This sort of shot, which doesn't give either player an advantage, is called a safety shot.

red, colour, and so on.

When a red ball is potted, it stays in the pocket. But while any reds remain on the table, any colour potted is returned to its spot. Once all the reds are off the table, the colours are potted in ascending order of value, from yellow to black. They are now left in the pockets and when the black is finally potted, the frame ends. The player or pair with most points wins the frame.

As well as points scored for potting balls, points can be given away for foul strokes. The minimum penalty for a foul is four points.

The commonest fouls and their penalties are:
● Missing a ball. Penalty: value of

▼ A wood or plastic triangle is used to position the reds at the start of a frame.

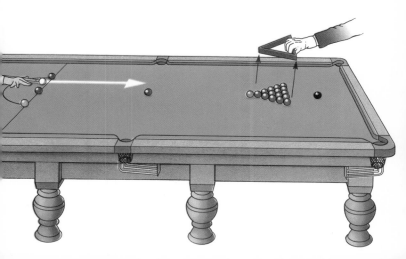

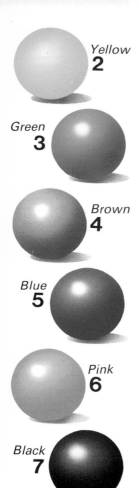

Yellow
2

Green
3

Brown
4

Blue
5

Pink
6

Black
7

▲ *These balls are known as the colours. They each have the value of points shown.*

the ball which was attempted (called the **ball on**).

- Hitting the wrong ball. Penalty: value of the ball hit or the ball on (whichever is greater).
- Pocketing the cue ball. Penalty: value of the ball on. When the cue ball is pocketed, the next player puts it back on the table and starts his break from anywhere within the D.

You can commit two or more fouls at once. For example, a player aiming for a red, may hit the blue and also pocket the white. There is only one penalty, which is always the highest. Here it would be five points, the value of the blue.

If a player hits the ball on first, it is not a foul if the cue ball then hits other balls. But it *is* a foul if the cue ball hits another ball before the ball on.

There are several other ways of committing fouls, a few of which are:

- Striking when balls are still moving.
- Striking with both feet off the floor.
- Hitting a ball off the table.
- Touching a ball with anything other than the tip of the cue.

- Using a ball other than the white as the cue ball.

Most players (and television watchers) know these basic rules, but there are a few interesting points which often crop up and are not always understood. Among them are:

Push stroke. If, instead of a clean strike, the cue stays in contact with the cue ball when it has started moving, this is a push stroke, and is a foul. It often happens that the cue ball and object ball are almost touching and the cue is still in contact with cue ball when the object ball is struck. This, too, is a push stroke.

Jump shot. If the cue ball is made to jump another ball, this is a foul. At one time it was legal, but not now.

Miss. A player must always attempt to hit the ball on. If the referee feels that he did not, he calls foul, awards the penalty and asks the other player if he wants the ball or balls to be replaced. The referee can then make the player retry the shot. This happens in championship matches where the miss is considered not so much

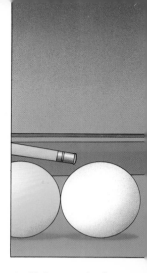

▲ *If the cue ball comes to rest touching another ball, the player must play away without touching the other ball.*

deliberate as of a poor standard. The non-striker almost always asks for the shot to be replayed.

Touching ball. If the cue ball comes to rest touching another ball, the player must 'play away' from that ball without touching it.

Free ball. If a player is **snookered** from a foul stroke, he is awarded a free ball. He can select any ball to hit. For example, if he is snookered on a red, he might nominate a blue. The blue becomes a 'red' for the purposes of the next shot. If he pots the blue, the score is one point and the blue is re-spotted on the table. Being 'snookered' means that you cannot hit the object ball in a straight line because there are other balls in the way.

Play again rule. A player cannot benefit from a foul. After a foul, the non-striker may request the player who fouled to play again from where the balls lie.

Respotted black. If, with only the black ball left, there are more than seven points between the players, it is usual not to play on, since one player cannot win. If there are seven points or less, play continues with the final score or

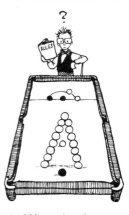

▲ We only give a summary of the rules of snooker in this book - enough to get you going. If you want the full rules, write off for a booklet to: Billiards and Snooker Control Council, Coronet House, Queen Street, Leeds LS1 2TN.

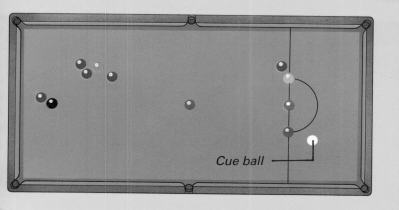

Cue ball

foul deciding the frame. If the scores are then equal, the black is put back on its spot, and players draw lots for first shot. The first player shoots from within the D, and the next score or foul ends the frame.

Spotting colours. When a colour is potted, and cannot be replaced because its spot is occupied, it is spotted on the highest value spot which is free. If all the spots are occupied, it is placed as near as possible to its own spot in a line to the top cushion.

▲ *The arrangement of balls shown here would normally be a good snooker – that is, the cue ball cannot 'see' any of the reds. But if the previous shot had been a foul, the player can nominate any ball as the ball on.*

4: Snooker action

When you line up a straight shot to pocket a red, say, it is easy to see the path the white must run to strike the object ball. It is not difficult to line the cue up to point directly along the line the cue ball must take.

What is difficult is keeping the cue exactly along that line when you draw it back and push it forward to strike. The secret of a successful cueing action is to get your stance right.

Stand firmly, with your legs apart. Your back leg (right if you are right-handed) should be rigid and at an angle to the line of the shot. Imagine the cue is pointing to 12 o'clock and point your right foot to about 2 o'clock. You should find the cue passes over your instep. Your body weight should be slightly forward, on the left leg.

The distance between your feet depends on your height. Have them where it's comfortable. Keep

▲ *Alex Higgins concentrates on a difficult shot.*

▶ *This is the best angle to play at – the right foot is at about 2 o'clock to the cue's 12 o'clock.*

both feet on the ground and don't move them during a stroke.

The third 'anchor' of your stance is the **bridging hand.** This is the hand you place on the table to support the cue. Stretch out your left arm as far as it will go. Your bridge-hand fingers should splay down on the cloth, which slightly raises the palm. Cock your thumb, with the base pressing into the cloth. The cue can now run smoothly between your forefinger and thumb. Most players like at least 25 cm (10 in) between bridging hand and cue ball. The more of the cue you can look along the easier it is to sight the shot correctly.

As with your feet, the bridging hand and arm remain locked steady during the shot. So does your head! The eye you sight with should be directly above the cue. Most players sight equally with both eyes, in which case the cue passes directly under your nose, but some players favour one eye – you might notice Rex Williams sighting with his left eye. Your chin should be nearly resting on the cue.

The cue itself should be as flat as possible, nearly parallel to the table top. With your legs, head and left arm locked, your right arm becomes the working part of the cue action.

With the tip of the cue 13 mm ($\frac{1}{2}$ in) from the cue ball, your right forearm should be vertical. This will show you where to grip the cue butt. If your cue is the correct

▲ Splay your fingers out like this to form a bridge. The cue then rests comfortably over your thumb.

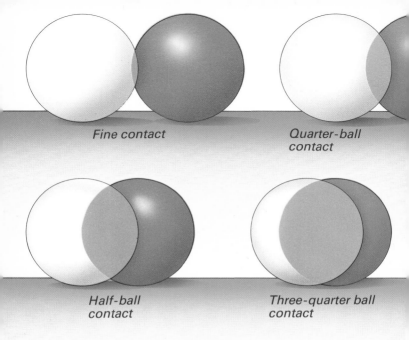

Fine contact

Quarter-ball contact

Half-ball contact

Three-quarter ball contact

▲ *The various 'contacts' are shown here with overlapping balls. A full ball contact sends the object ball straight ahead. The other contacts make the object ball move off at various angles.*

length, your hand should grip the butt at the end.

Your grip should not be tight, but just firm enough to keep the cue under control.

In making the shot, the right elbow acts like a hinge. The cue is drawn back by the hinge opening, the cue being kept as flat as possible. The cue is then pushed forward by the hinge closing, and

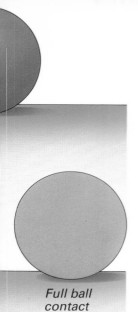

Full ball contact

the tip drives through the ball and then follows the shot on through.

Nothing else should move while your right arm pushes the cue forward. Beginners are inclined to raise their heads too early, to see if the **object ball** is heading towards the pocket. Watch Steve Davis. Notice how his head remains still, how far his cue follows through and how long he remains down after the shot before he stands up.

You can master the basic stance, but you won't pot a ball unless you can aim correctly. Where the cue ball and object ball are in line with the pocket the aiming line is obvious. You aim the cue ball to hit the object ball full on.

If the object ball has to be struck to travel at an angle into a pocket, then the cue ball must hit the object ball at less than full on.

Here is a tip to help you work out the point of contact between the cue and object balls. Imagine a second cue ball touching the object ball and in line with a pocket. If you now strike the actual cue ball so that it will 'hit' the imaginary cue ball full on, then the object ball should go towards the pocket.

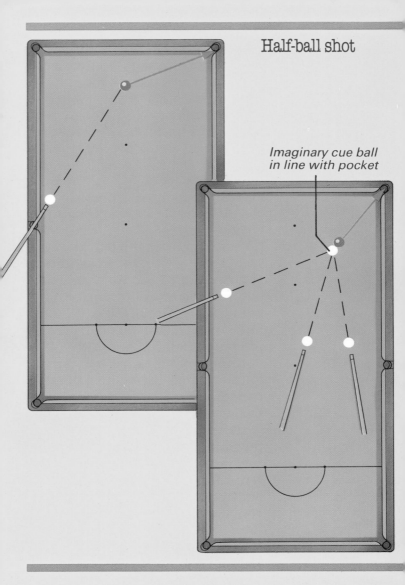

Half-ball shot

Imaginary cue ball in line with pocket

◀ This picture shows a typical half-ball shot. If the cue ball hits the object ball on its left-hand side, then it will head towards the corner pocket.

◀ *This picture shows a typical half-ball shot. If the cue ball hits the object ball on its left-hand side, then it will head towards the corner pocket.*

◀ *To hit an object ball at the correct angle, imagine a second ball dead in line with it, pointing towards the pocket. Aim for full contact with the imaginary ball, and you should get the ball down.*

Three cues and angles are shown here, but the idea is the same wherever you aim from.

Often, the ball positions will not allow you to place your bridging hand firmly on the table and you will have to make do. The looped bridge is useful for this. Your forefinger loops over the cue, which is pushed through the loop over thumb and middle finger.

This bridge is particularly useful for shots near the cushion. Here, three fingers can press onto the table while the palm rests on the cushion.

Often the cushion itself can be used as part of the bridge, with the cue partly resting on it, but still controlled by your thumb and fingers. Do not grip the cue. It must slide easily.

When you start to line up a shot, look at the object ball. When you are comfortably settled into your stance, move your eyes to the cue ball and check that everything is lined up correctly. You will probably look from cue to object ball several times before you strike, but remember to move your eyes only, not your head. When you actually strike the cue ball, you should be looking at the contact point on the object ball.

5: Screw, stun and side

Controlling the cue ball is one of the big requirements for snooker success. Control is gained with various forms of spin, given by hitting the cue ball off-centre.

If it did not matter where the cue ball went after hitting the object ball, you would simply strike the cue ball in the middle. But you always want it to stop in a good position from which to pot another ball, and this is almost always off at an angle, elsewhere on the table.

To get the cue ball to spin, you have to hit it at different points on its surface.

Imagine the cue ball has a clock face, as shown on the right. Striking at 12 o'clock gives forward, or top, spin. When it hits an object ball, the cue ball will 'follow through' after impact, gradually slowing down.

If the cue ball is hit mid-way between 12 o'clock and centre, there will be some follow through,

▶ *Hitting the cue ball at different 'clock points' makes it spin and helps you control it.*

Hitting the cue ball

Top spin

Stun and screw

Side

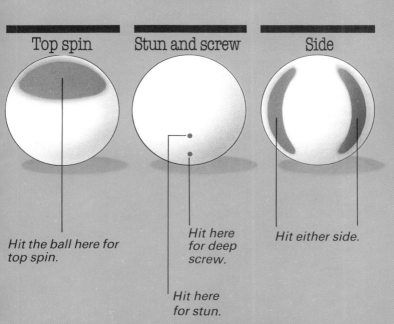

Hit the ball here for top spin.

Hit here for deep screw.

Hit here for stun.

Hit either side.

but not as much as before. So the amount of follow through can be varied depending on how high you hit the ball. The strength of your shot also has its effect!

Stun shots are the reverse of follow through shots. Hitting the cue ball just below the centre gives slight back-spin. Impact with the object ball stops the cue ball dead – called 'stunned'.

Striking the cue ball near the bottom will cause even more back-spin, and the cue ball will come back after impact. This is known as **screw**. Striking the cue ball hard at 6 o'clock will make the ball come back very strongly. This is known as 'deep screw'.

If the cue ball strikes the object ball at an angle, it is impossible to stop the cue ball dead. In this case stun will prevent it from running as far as normal, while top spin or screw will alter the angle it leaves the object ball. For example, if the object ball is struck on the right, the cue ball will always go to the right, but with top spin it will go forwards as well, while with screw it will go right but also backwards.

So provided that he is potting

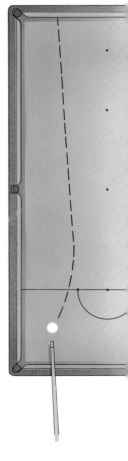

▲ *This picture shows the path of a 9 o'clock swerve shot.*

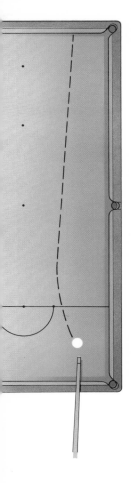

the object ball at an angle, the expert can make the cue ball go in many directions, an art known as cue ball control.

With each of these shots you have to keep the cue as flat as possible – screw shots are not played just by lowering the tip. A screw is played with more power than usual and it helps to move your bridging hand nearer the cue ball, perhaps 15–20 cm (6–8 in) away. You should also grip the butt that much further forward.

You must also lower your bridge. Turn your bridge hand so that the weight of your body is on the base of the thumb, while your little finger should just touch the cloth.

Just as the cue ball can be made to travel backwards and forwards with screw and top-spin, so it can be controlled with **side**, or side-spin.

If the cue ball is struck with a left-hand side (the tip hits the ball at 9 o'clock) the immediate effect is to push the ball out to the right. Gradually, the spin bites on the cloth and the ball curves back to

▲ *Here you see the path of a 3 o'clock swerve shot.*

the left. The harder the ball is hit, the longer it takes for the spin to bite.

A **swerve shot** like this is played mainly to get out of a snooker or to pot a ball right on the edge of a pocket which cannot be reached directly. Although easy to play, swerves are difficult to control.

Swerve shots are played with the butt of the cue raised and are exaggerated side shots.

Side used with the normal cue action works in the same way, but the swerve is too slight to notice. The shot is used to alter the angle the cue ball makes when it leaves the cushion.

▼ *These pictures show the different rebound paths a cue ball will take if you use side when you hit it.*

If you hit it correctly, the object ball goes into the pocket with both the shots shown here.

The shot below is an example of running side.

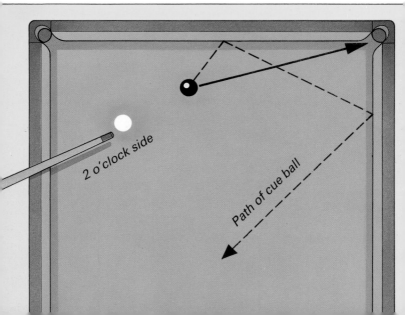

2 o'clock side

Path of cue ball

Striking the cue ball on one side will widen the angle and take the cue ball away (called 'running side') while striking on the other side will narrow the angle (called 'check side').

Using side is complicated and takes years of practice to perfect.

Joe Davis and Eddie Charlton both give the same advice to beginners, 'Don't use side'. It is sound advice – master the basics first. But you can see the pros using it on television, so it's useful to understand the basic idea, and to get in some practice.

▼ *Here, the cue ball is made to follow a much steeper angle down the table.*
This is called check side.

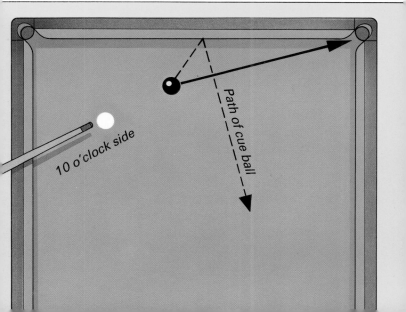

10 o'clock side

Path of cue ball

6: Plant shots

A plant, sometimes called a **set**, is the potting of a ball by playing one object ball onto another. Usually two balls are involved but, in theory, plants can be made with any number.

The commonest form of plant happens when two object balls are touching. More difficult ones are achieved when there is space between the balls. Plants are usually played only when a direct pot is impossible.

The simplest plant is when two object balls are touching and they are in line with a pocket. A full contact with the nearest object ball will send the other ball into the pocket.

A plant shot is also possible when the two balls are not quite in line. Here the back object ball must be hit at less than full contact to push the front ball at the correct angle. The pictures on the next two pages show a number of plants.

▶ *Typical plant, shots like this one are fairly easy, provided you take them carefully and make sure you hit the ball at the correct angle.*

You can sometimes play a plant shot in which the back, or nearest, object ball is the one to be potted. Setting up the balls and practising the shot will show just how straightforward this shot is (see picture 2) – it does not even require any great accuracy with the cue ball. Hit the object ball on the correct side and it will go in.

If the balls are not touching, as in picture 3, then imagine the nearest ball to be the cue ball, and play it onto the other object ball.

Sometimes there might not be a direct pot and no easy plants. However a close look might show an object ball which can be played in, off another ball. An example is shown in picture 4. A three or even four-ball plant, such as that shown in picture 5, is spectacular and satisfying.

Always look out for possible plants. It is annoying if an opponent pots a ball with a simple plant which you failed to spot! Opportunities for plants often happen near the beginning of a game, when there are plenty of reds clustered together, sometimes directly in line to a pocket.

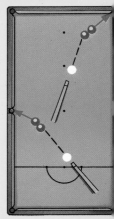

1. *Balls not quite in line with pockets.*

Plant shots

Here are some typical types of plant shot. Watch out for them on the table and don't let the other player steal any from you

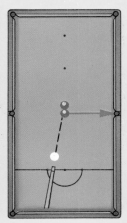

2. Potting a red at right-angles to a pocket.

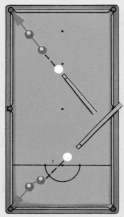

3. A plant with the reds well apart.

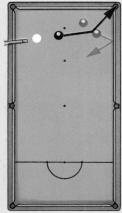

4. Black potted in off the red.

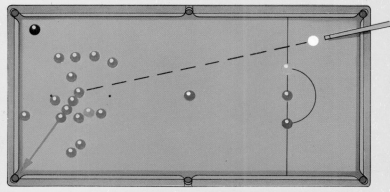

5. Four-ball plant with all the balls on the table.

7: Using the rest

Sometimes the cue ball is in a difficult spot on the table and you can't use your bridging hand. This is when you have to use a rest.

The style of rest most often used is shown below. It can be turned to form a 'shallow vee' or a 'high vee'. The shallow vee is used for most shots. With the rest about 20 cm (8 in) from the cue ball, the cue can be positioned on the shallow vee at its natural angle, to strike the ball dead-centre. Use the high vee when above-centre striking is needed.

▶ Use a rest whenever you can't reach the ball properly.

▼ The standard rest can be used in both a high vee and a shallow vee position.

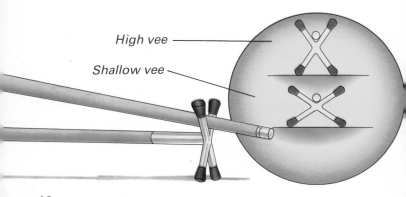

High vee

Shallow vee

The cueing action when using the rest is different from normal. The rest itself lies on the table. Keep it steady with your left hand, with your elbow on the table. The position of your feet is not important – just make sure you are comfortable.

Grip the cue at the end of the butt, supporting it with your thumb. Most players bring the first two fingers over the top of the butt, with the bent third finger resting against it. Some players prefer to bring just one finger over.

Hold the cue just below eye-level, so the whole length of it can be used for sighting. The cue action is now a push with the wrist and forearm. Thumb and fingers give delicate control and you should follow through to make sure the cue keeps straight.

▲ *The half-butt rest is used for an extra-long reach down the table.*

The half-butt is a long rest about 3 metres (9 ft) long. It is used for shots where a player has to reach almost the whole length of the table.

The half-butt comes with a special long cue. The top pros prefer to use cue extensions, which enable them to use their own cues.

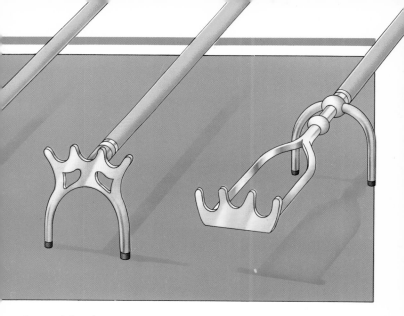

The spider is a rest with a high bridge. This lets you aim the cue above any balls which might be in the way. Sometimes an extended spider may be necessary if there are lots of obstructing balls, but this doesn't happen very often.

▲ *The spider and extended spider are used to let a player aim over balls that are in the way of the cue ball.*

Using a rest ought – in theory – to be more difficult than taking an ordinary shot. Most players find it takes a lot more concentration to hit the ball just right.

In the long run, it is easier to learn to use the rest with confidence than to practice contortions to avoid using it.

8: Tactics to win

If you are playing in a match, make sure you arrive in plenty of time – there's nothing worse than being flustered because you are in a hurry. Make sure you are comfortably dressed, so you can forget about everything except the game.

It will help you to relax if you think of matches as a form of practice. Don't be afraid of using the shots you have been practising. Even if they go wrong and cost you frames at first, you will get good match experience.

Concentrate on every shot and play as if you mean to win. Even if you have some unlucky strokes, remember you will probably hit a lucky streak sooner or later, so don't get too depressed.

When deciding between playing a safety shot or trying for a pot, remember that a game cannot be won on safety shots alone. Sooner or later you have to pot the balls to win. It usually pays to be positive.

▶ Joe Johnson, in his championship game against Steve Davis. Part of a pro's success comes from good tactics and being able to choose the right shot for any situation.

▲ Don't be late for the match!

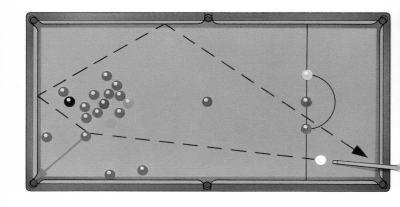

Most frames begin with both players concentrating on bringing the cue ball back to the **baulk** line for safety, so as not to allow the next player an easy chance at a pot. If you can be certain of leaving your opponent a difficult shot, don't hesitate to split up the reds a little. It makes it harder for your opponent to play safe in his turn.

Always visualize the completed shot. Work out where all the balls will go and be aware of the possibility of a 'double-kiss'. This is what happens if the cue ball and object ball make contact twice, usually after one has rebounded from a cushion. Know the path you intend the cue ball to take to safety

▲ *In this shot the players aims the cue ball to return back to baulk – a safety shot which doesn't give the other player an easy chance to pot a ball.*

On the way, the ball has a 'free' chance of potting a red. This is called a shot to nothing.

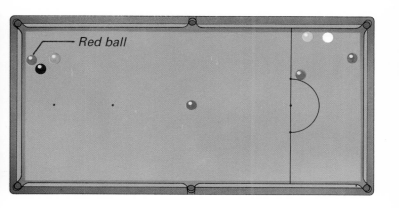

Red ball

and think about what might happen if your shot is inaccurate. Know the margin for error, and if it is too fine, look for another shot.

Keep watch for the 'shot to nothing'. This is where you can combine a safety shot with a 'free' attempt at a pot. The picture above left shows such a shot.

Be aware of the score, but don't be over confident if you are 40 points in front, or gloomy if 40 points behind. If you need those 40 points to win, with the last red on the table, think of the value of a free ball. One good snooker, as shown, could earn a free ball. This, followed by a black, still leaves 35 points – so you can win.

▲ *This is an example of a good snooker – it is difficult enough to hit the red, let alone leave it safe.*

9: Practice shots and tricks

Practice makes perfect, particularly in snooker. It is a game in which you can't be interfered with – you cannot be tripped, thumped or hit. And how you perform depends largely on how hard you have practised.

Concentrate on each shot while practising and if you miss a shot, replace the balls and play it again. Find out where you went wrong and get it right next time.

The first thing to get right is your cueing action. Place the cue ball on the brown spot, then play it up the table. Aim it to pass over the blue, pink and black spots, returning back over them again, including the brown. If it veers off, then you are putting side on the ball, your stance is wrong or you are moving as you make the shot.

Practise straight potting from various distances. A good long shot is to pot the blue from its spot

▶ *Making a break with the reds in a line is good practice and makes a change. In this picture, some of the reds have already been potted. Space the reds about 50 mm (2 in) apart.*

▲ *If you get bored, take a break rather than fall asleep.*

into a top pocket with the cue ball in baulk.

Put the colours on their spots and pot them from various angles.

Another good practice is to put the black on its spot and to pot it as many times as possible, returning it to its spot each time, by playing the cue ball from where it comes to rest.

Lining up the balls is popular. Space all the object balls in a line from pink to brown spots. Then pot them, in any order, but don't disturb any balls except the one you are potting. When you are good at this, you can make it harder by not allowing the cue ball to touch a cushion.

Another line-up practice is to put the colours on their spots, lining up the reds in the middle. The idea is to make a normal break, but not disturbing the line of reds as you pot the balls. Just pick off the reds, one by one, until they are all down.

Keep scores on all these routines so you can keep a check on your progress. Setting targets and beating them keeps up interest – practice shouldn't get boring!

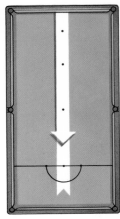

▲ Use this routine to check your cueing action – the ball should move in a dead straight line.

▶ Here are some trick shots. They are fun to do and impressive to watch.

Trick shots/1: The Zig-Zag

The aim of this trick is to pot the black after making contact with the reds.

Line up the reds and place the black and cue ball as shown on the right. Strike the cue ball with 4 o'clock side. Aim for the cushion just before the first red. When the angle is correct, the ball will bounce back and forth between each red and the cushion, potting the black at the end.

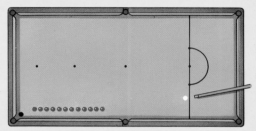

▲ *Setting up the shot*

▼ *How it works when you make the shot. It needs to be a hefty power stroke.*

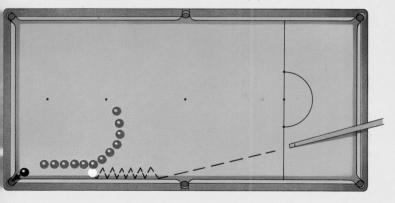

Trick 2: Four reds in one

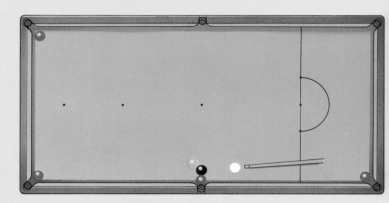

Place the balls as shown. Black touches red, in line with the centre pocket. Yellow touches black, in line between black and red at top-left. Cue ball is 20 cm (8 in) from black.

Hit the cue ball with 6 o'clock deep screw full on the black. The black and yellow should pot three of the reds. The cue ball screws back to pot the last red in the bottom right hand pocket.

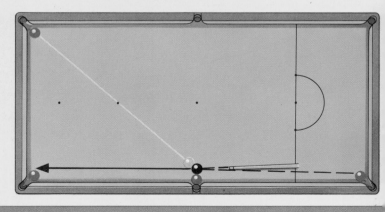

Trick 3: The blue mystery

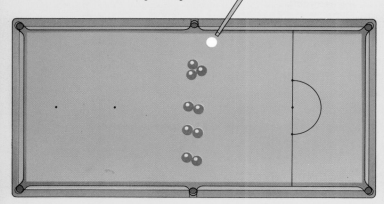

Set up the balls as shown above. The left-hand reds are in line with the side of the pocket. The others aim at the middle. The red-blue-red cluster all touch.

Strike the cue ball dead-centre for half-ball contact on the first red, cannoning off into the blue. The first red goes away, while the others clear the way for the blue to roll into the pocket!

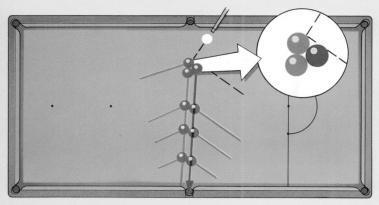

10: Billiards

Billiards was the forerunner of snooker, and is played on the same table. Many top snooker players also play billiards, and a knowledge of the game is a help to any snooker player.

The game (strictly called English billiards) is played with one red ball and two cue balls – one is plain white, one has a black spot. Each player, or team in pairs, has one of the cue balls. Players strike only their own ball.

Play starts with the red ball on the 'spot' – the same spot for the black in snooker. The first player plays from **in-hand**, this is from anywhere within the D. The first player continues to play until he fails to score. The second player then takes a turn. Each player's completed turn is called a break as in snooker.

Points are scored as shown on page 56. They can be scored in combination – hazards and

▶ These are the basic ways of scoring shots at billiards. The balls don't have to go in these particular pockets.

The first player can only score with the red and his own white, as the other white ball only comes onto the table when the other player starts the game.

Scoring shots at billiards

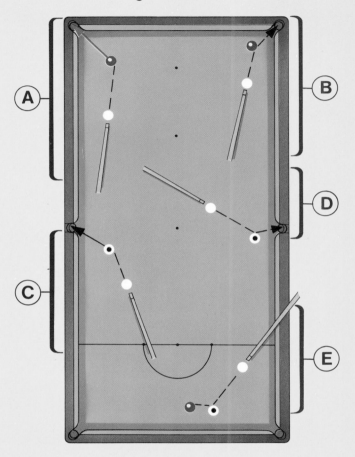

A: Pot red   B: In-off red   C: Pot white object ball
D: In-off white object ball   E: Cannon

Points are scored for these strokes:

Cannons. When the cue ball strikes both other balls, a cannon is scored and is worth two points.

Hazards. There are four kinds of hazard:

- *Potting the red scores 3 points. The red is replaced on its spot.*
- *Potting the opponent's cue ball, scores two points. Opponent's cue ball stays off the table.*
- *In-off the red (pocketing the cue ball after hitting the red), scores three points.*
- *In-off opponent's cue ball, scores two points.*

In the last two cases the striker plays the cue ball from in-hand. Pots are often called winning hazards.

cannons made on the same stroke both count. Where the cue ball is pocketed after a cannon, the hazard scores three if the red was struck first, two if the white. The most points possible on one stroke is ten – a cannon striking red first and all three balls going into pockets. This is not necessarily a good shot, however, as it almost certainly means the end of the break.

At one time there was no restriction on the number of times each shot could be made in succession, so players got all three balls near a cushion and made endless cannons. These breaks sometimes lasted not hours but weeks. A player called Tom Reece once made 499,135 cannons, taking over five weeks!

The game became boring, and restrictions were introduced. Now only 15 hazards may be scored consecutively. To continue a break after that, the striker must make a cannon. This is impossible if the opponent's cue ball is off the table. In this case, it is put on the table on the middle (brown) spot of the D or, if occupied, on the right-hand (yellow) spot.

▲ *Enough of the rules of billiards are included here for you to play a game. If you want the complete rules, write to the Billiards and Snooker Control Council. The address is given on page 20.*

If the red is potted twice in succession from its spot, it is put on the centre spot. If this is occupied it goes on the pyramid (pink) spot.

There are also limits on the number of cannons allowed. After 75, the striker must make a hazard to continue.

Fouls give two points to the other side and end the break. If a player hits no ball in a shot, that is a foul. There are many others, similar to those in snooker, including jump shots and forcing balls off the table.

If the striker's cue ball ends up touching another ball after a shot, the red is placed on its spot. The opponent's ball, if it is on the table, is put on the centre spot and the striker starts the next shot from in-hand.

The winner is either the first past a set number of points or the player ahead after an agreed time limit.

From 1985, the Billiards World Championship has been decided on a 'best of five' games, each of 300 points or more. This system keeps up audience interest and provides lots of climaxes. The average break is 25, with centuries (100 points) and double centuries not uncommon.

In billiards, follow-through top-spin shots are the ones you need to use most. The in-off losing hazard is a basic stroke. To get a big break, you have to control three balls compared with two in snooker. Because cue ball control is important, playing billiards should help your snooker playing.

But billiards is a good game to play anyway and the most popular way to build up a break is the 'top of the table' play, shown in the pictures on the right. All three balls are brought near the red spot. Delicate cannons are played, with the occasional losing hazard and pots of the red. If you get it right, you can keep the play going for a long time. One possible sequence is shown in the drawings.

The half-ball losing hazard is such an important shot in billiards it is a must for practice. With the red on the centre spot you should be able to go in-off a top pocket from in hand (i.e. placing the cue ball anywhere in baulk). Keep practising it until you are perfect.

This is a good exercise in very careful and precise ball control. If you can keep playing a sequence like this, you can repeat the moves for as long as you like.

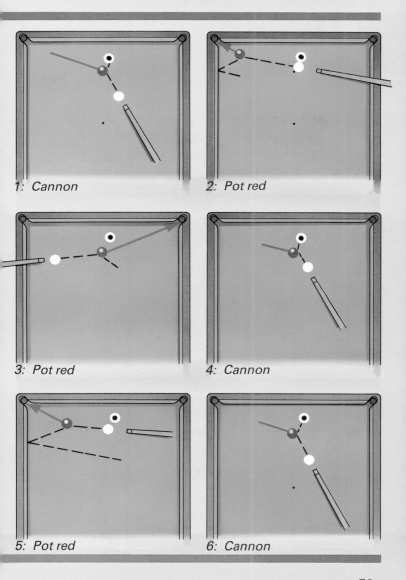

1: Cannon

2: Pot red

3: Pot red

4: Cannon

5: Pot red

6: Cannon

11: Pool

Pool is played in several ways. The game is most popular in the United States, where they play a version called '14.1 continuous play'. In Britain, a version of the 'eight-ball' game is played, usually on a smaller table and with different balls.

▶ *This is the table used in America. Racked balls are laid out with the point of the triangle on the foot spot.*

14.1 Continuous play
This is played with 15 numbered object balls and a white cue ball. Eight of the balls are plain colours,

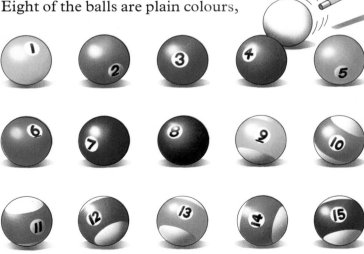

14.1 Standard American table

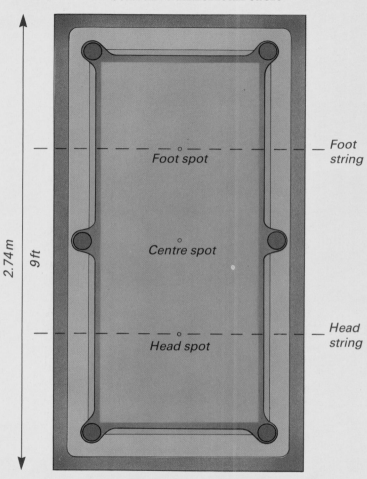

2.74 m

9 ft

Foot string

Foot spot

Centre spot

Head string

Head spot

▲ In 14.1 pool, the balls are racked in this order.

the other seven are striped.

The object balls are racked in a triangle in the order shown on the left. The 15 ball lies on the 'foot' spot. A player's aim is to be first to score an agreed number of points.

A point is scored by pocketing a 'called' ball into a 'called' pocket. A striker must say before each shot which ball he intends to pot into which pocket. If the shot is successful, any other balls pocketed in the same stroke also score a point.

The break starts by playing the cue ball from behind the head string. If a called ball goes into a called pocket, the break continues. Otherwise you drive the cue ball and two object balls to a cushion, and your opponent plays from where the balls lie.

If you drive two object balls to hit a cushion but 'scratch' the cue ball into a pocket, you lose a point and your turn ends. If you fail to get any of these things, you have fouled and lose two points. Your opponent can play from where the balls lie or ask you to start again, with the balls reframed and playing from in-hand. This can be repeated until you meet the obligations. You lose two points each time you fail.

A break continues while you keep scoring. It ends when you miss the shot called. Pocketed object balls are returned to the table when only one is left. If you pot a cue ball your turn ends and you get a one-point penalty. The next striker plays from in-hand.

Play is continuous in pool. When the 14th object ball is potted, the 15th is left in position as the 'break ball'. The cue ball is left in position and the 14 pocketed balls are racked, with the space left by the break ball at the foot spot. The break continues as usual.

Eight-ball Pool

In this game, there are two groups of coloured object balls. During the game each player gets one of the groups, and the winner has to pocket his own group of object balls, then the black ball. A player who pockets the black ball while any of his own balls are on the table loses immediately.

The first player breaks off by striking the cue ball from any point within the D. For the shot to be

▼ *Balls are racked like this in eight-ball pool. The black is often called the 8-ball, because it is the eighth one to be potted.*

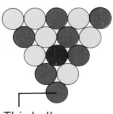

This ball goes on the head spot.

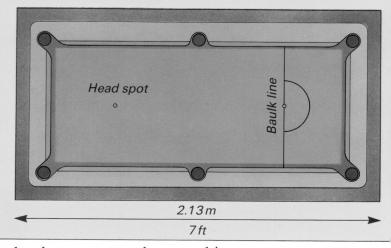

Head spot

Baulk line

2.13 m

7 ft

legal you must pocket any object ball or drive two or more to hit a cushion. If you don't do this, your opponent can accept the balls as they lie, or order a rerack.

▲ *The standard British table is smaller than the one used in America. The cues are shorter too.*

Players continue alternately until an object ball is potted. If you pot a ball, you adopt its colour as your group. You continue the turn (called a 'visit') until you fail to pot a ball of your own colour or you commit a foul. If, before you have your groups, anyone pockets a ball from each group in the same shot, he can choose which group to have.

If a foul is committed, the offender misses a turn – his

opponent has two visits. Also, on the first shot (and the first shot only) after a foul, normal rules are suspended and the striker can play any ball, even potting balls of his opponent, but not the black. This is called a 'free table'. Any other pot gained in this shot is legal and he continues his turn, still being on the first visit.

A player snookered on a foul stroke can pick up the cue ball and play from the D.

Foul strokes are severely punished, as the player who has two visits usually attempts to clear his colours and the black to win. Otherwise, the game is often tactical, with neither player attempting necessarily to pot balls, but rather to leave them on the edge of pockets, to pot when required. At the same time they block the pockets to the other player.

If a player 'goes for home' but fails to pot the last ball, it is easy for an opponent with, say, six balls on the table, to produce a good snooker. From the two visits which could result he could easily win the game. So the game becomes a nice battle of tactics.

Eight-ball fouls

You foul if:

- *You pocket the cue ball.*
- *You miss a ball.*
- *You hit the black or your opponent's ball before your own.*
- *You pot any of your opponent's balls.*

12: Great players of today

In professional snooker, each season begins with a ranking list. It is based on the performances in the six open tournaments of the two previous seasons. Anybody can enter an open tournament. At the end of each season, the points won are added to those of the previous season to give a ranking list for the next year.

Players are seeded in each tournament so that the best avoid each other until the later stages. So that the seeding is not the same for all tournaments throughout the season, the holder of a trophy is seeded number 1, and the other seeds are ranked from the list.

Being seeded in the first 16 gives automatic entry to the 16-player Masters Championship, and exemption from qualifying in the World Championship. In fact, these players are currently guaranteed over £10,000 per year in 'winnings', even if they do not win a match!

▲ The World Championship trophy is the target for all pro snooker players. Each season begins with the players being seeded. This is a system of choosing players so that all the best ones don't play each other in early matches – so the really big games come late in the tournament.

The top world players

Steve Davis

Was born in Britain on 22 August, 1957, and turned pro in 1978. He really came to the front in 1980/1 when he beat Alex Higgins in the Coral UK Open. He won the World Championship but crashed in the first round in 1982, to everyone's surprise. Since then he has won it twice more.

Cliff Thorburn

Was born in Canada on 16 January, 1948, and is one of the steadiest players in snooker. He has been a professional player since 1973 and was World Champion in 1980. He is called 'the grinder' because he never gives up and wears down his opponents in long sessions.

Dennis Taylor
Comes from Northern Ireland, and was born on 19 January, 1949. A pro player since 1971, he didn't win a major title until 1984. He then got special glasses, which have since become his trademark. They are specially made so he can look comfortably at the ball while he has his head down.

Tony Knowles
Hit the headlines when he beat Steve Davis in 1982. He was born in Britain on 13 June, 1955. Though he has the talent, he has generally failed to turn it to major matchwinning skill. He is currently number four in the championship rankings.

Jimmy White
Was born in Britain on 2 May, 1962, and was the youngest ever English amateur champ at 16. He was the youngest-world amateur champ at 18, and at 19, was the youngest winner of a pro tournament. He is left-handed, and just about the quickest player around the table.

Alex Higgins
Was born in Northern Ireland on 18 March, 1949. Higgins is nicknamed the 'Hurricane'. He is a bad boy of the game, often at odds with the authorities. But he plays well, and often has patches of sheer genius which makes his game exciting for people to watch.

Willie Thorne

Was born in Britain on 4 March 1954 and has been called a 'world best' player, but one whose nerves let him down in an important match. Winning a major match in 1984 changed his image a little, but he still loses too often to players not as good as himself. He is now seventh in the rankings.

Joe Johnson

Has a similar 'nervy' reputation to Willie Thorne. But he beat his dislike of live TV cameras to become the surprise World Champion in 1986. He was born in Britain on 29 July, 1952, and still claims he is better at singing than at playing snooker!

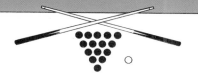

The 1986/7 world ranking list

Here are the top 16 players in 1986/7.
The previous year's rankings are
shown in brackets.

1 Steve Davis (1)

2 Cliff Thorburn (2)

3 Dennis Taylor (4)

4 Tony Knowles (3)

5 Jimmy White (7)

6 Alex Higgins (9)

7 Willie Thorn (11)

8 Joe Johnson (16)

9 Kirk Stevens (5)

10 Terry Griffiths (8)

11 Tony Meo (10)

12 Silvino Francisco (13)

13 Neal Foulds (23)

14 Doug Mountjoy (15)

15 Ray Reardon (6)

16 Rex Williams (27)

Rising Stars

26 Peter Francisco (59)

30 Barry West

37 Tony Drago

51 Stephen Hendry

13: The international season

Professional snooker players keep themselves busy all through the year. In the summer some coach at hotels, some give exhibition matches, and most combine both coaching and exhibitions. With the rapid spread of snooker around the world many of the leading professionals now make overseas trips to promote the game.

The British tournament season starts in September with the Scottish Masters which has been played in Glasgow since 1981. Steve Davis performed a hat-trick here from 1982 to 1984.

Most years one or two events are discontinued and new ones take their place, but a regular circuit of around 15 major tournaments has built up over the last few seasons. All lead to the climax of the World Professional Championship, starting at the Crucible Theatre, Sheffield, towards the end of April.

▲ *Joe Johnson and Steve Davis battled it out for victory in the 1986 Snooker World Championship final. Johnson won 18–12.*

Joe Johnson's surprise £70,000 victory in 1986 was an exciting match, as was Dennis Taylor's win the year before. Ray Reardon, Terry Griffiths, Steve Davis, Cliff Thorburn and Alex Higgins are all past world champions.

The World Cup is played in March by teams of three from different countries. It has been won since 1979 by Wales, England, Canada and Ireland.

14: Snooker facts and records

It is a player's responsibility to make sure all the balls are correctly placed before the start of a game.

The referee must not warn of any possible fouls if a ball is wrongly placed.

In 1938, a player called Alec Brown was faced with a difficult shot – the cue ball was buried in a pack of reds. Brown put his hand in his pocket and pulled out a mini-cue, just 12 cm (4½ in) long! He played his shot, but the referee didn't think it was in the spirit of the game and Brown was promptly penalized.

The rules were quickly changed, and now cues must be at least 91 cm (3 ft) long.

Chalk was first used on cue tips about 1820. A player called John Carr claimed it was the secret of the then new screw shot.

Cliff Thorburn's maximum break in the 1983 World Professional Championship won him £10,000. It began with a lucky fluke. He missed a red into a top pocket, but it ran along the cushion into the opposite pocket.

Snooker nearly died out in the 1950s as few people were interested in the game. Fred Davis was World Champion until 1957, but he didn't think it was worth competing any more!

Joe Davis won £6.50 when he clinched the first World Championship in 1927. He gave up the title in 1946.

In the 20 years he held the title, he was unbeaten. He played with an old cue he bought for $37\frac{1}{2}$ pence.

There is no such thing as a tie in snooker – if players have level scores, the black is respotted.

World Champion Joe Johnson has always wanted to be a pop singer. He made a record, though it didn't get to number one in the charts.

Snooker rules allow for colour-blind players. The referee, though not normally allowed to give advice or opinions, can tell a player the colour of a ball, if asked.

At Bristol University, a team of researchers is working on a snooker – playing robot. At the moment the machine can pot reds and the colours.

The research team hope that within two years, they will have taught the robot the rules and some tactics.

Once they are convinced of the robot's prowess, it will appear on TV in matches against top professionals.

The research team hope their work will lead to more effective industrial robots for work in factories.

The two-piece cue has been around since 1950, when Canadian professional George Chenier used one. He beat the world tournament break record with a score of 144. Two-piece cues were popular again in the 1970s.

15: Glossary

Here are the meanings of most of the special snooker words used in this book.

Angled
If the cue ball cannot hit any part of a ball because it is obstructed by a corner of a cushion, it is said to be angled. If a cue ball is angled after a foul, the referee states 'angled ball' and the striker may play from in-hand.

Ball on
The object ball which a player is intending to hit in any particular shot.

Baulk
The area of the table between the bottom cushion and the baulk line.

Break
A player's turn. Also the sequence of scoring shots in a turn, and the score made from it. The first player is said to 'break-off'.

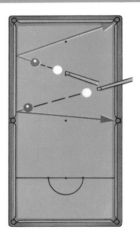

▲ *This picture shows two examples of balls being doubled across the table, off cushions and into pockets.*

Bridge or bridging hand
The hand which supports the cue during a stroke.

Cue ball
The white ball which is struck by the cue.

D
The part of the table inside the semicircle by the baulk line.

Double
Potting a ball into a pocket off one or more cushions.

Frame
The period of play between setting up the balls and potting them all. (See Game.)

Free ball
If a player is snookered from a foul, the referee calls 'free ball', giving the striker the option of nominating any ball as the ball on. It has the value of the ball on.

Game
A game is made up of an agreed number of frames. The World Championship final is made up of 35 frames.

In-hand
If the cue ball is pocketed or forced off the table, it is regarded as in-hand until played from the D by the next striker.

Jump shot
A foul shot where the cue ball jumps over another ball. There is no foul if it hits the ball on first.

Object ball
One of the 15 reds or six colours. The ball which the cue ball is intended to hit.

On
A ball which may be

lawfully hit by the first
impact of the cue ball is a
ball which is 'on'.

Plant
Two or more balls
arranged so that a pot can
be achieved by playing
one on to another.

Pot
Playing an object ball into
a pocket.

Push stroke
When the cue keeps in
contact with the cue ball
after it begins to move
forward or while the ball
strikes an object ball. It is
a foul shot.

Run through
A stroke which makes the
cue ball keep moving
after hitting an object
ball. It can also be the
result of such a stroke.

Screw
Back-spin put on to a cue

ball making it come back
after hitting with the
object ball.

Set
Another name for a plant.

Side
Side-spin put on to a cue
ball to affect the angle at
which it will bounce off
the cushion.

Snooker
When you cannot hit any
object ball in a straight
line. Ways around a
snooker usually involve
carefully calculated
shots, bouncing the cue
ball off one or more
cushions.

Stun
Back-spin put on the cue
ball so it stops dead when
it hits the object ball.

Swerve
Side-spin put on the cue
ball to make it curve.

Index

Acknowledgements

Illustrated by
Rhoda and Robert Burns
Peter Stevenson

Photographs supplied by
Colorsport
David Jefferis

Text editing by
Angela Royston

Many thanks to Peter Wilson
and the Dollimore family for
their help with specially posed
photographs.

Designed and edited
by Sunrise Books